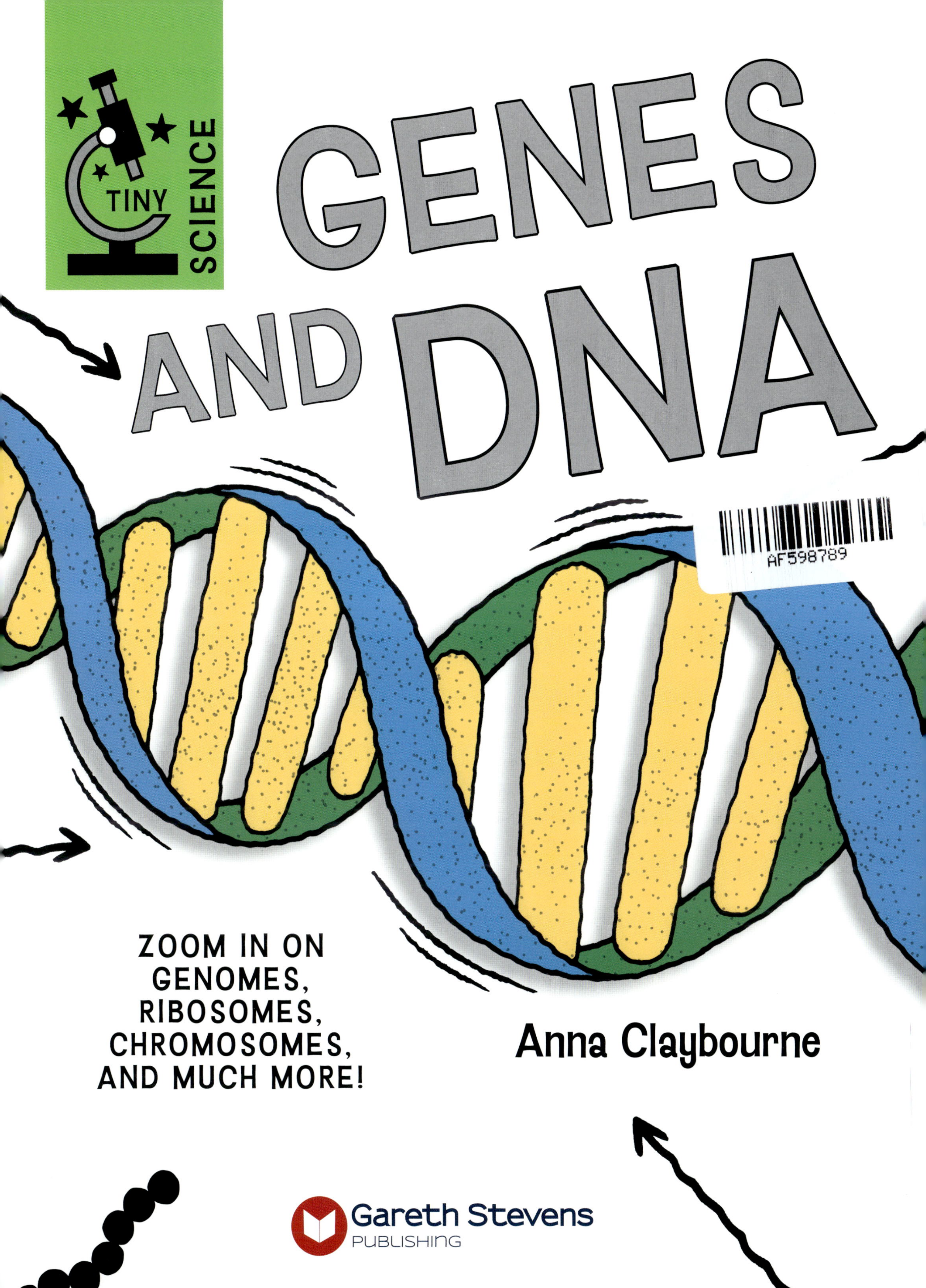
TINY SCIENCE
GENES AND DNA
AF598789
ZOOM IN ON
GENOMES,
RIBOSOMES,
CHROMOSOMES,
AND MUCH MORE!
Anna Claybourne
Gareth Stevens
PUBLISHING

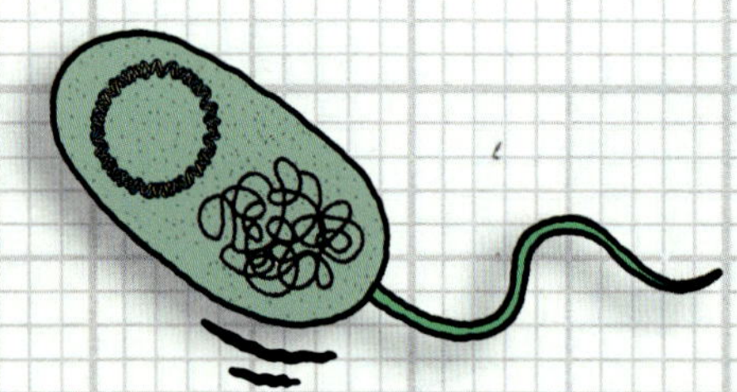

**Please visit our website,
www.garethstevens.com.
For a free color catalog of all
our high-quality books, call
toll free 1-800-542-2595 or
fax 1-877-542-2596.**

Published in 2025 by
Gareth Stevens Publishing
2544 Clinton St.
Buffalo, NY 14224

First published in Great Britain in 2022 by Wayland

Editor:
Grace Glendinning

Design and illustrations:
Matt Lilly

Cover design:
Matt Lilly

Cataloging-in-Publication Data

Names: Claybourne, Anna.
Title: Genes and DNA / Anna Claybourne.
Description: Buffalo, NY : Gareth Stevens Publishing, 2025. | Series: Tiny science | Includes glossary and index.
Identifiers: ISBN 9781538294116 (pbk.) | ISBN 9781538294123 (library bound) | ISBN 9781538294130 (ebook)
Subjects: LCSH: Genetics--Juvenile literature. | Genes--Juvenile literature. | DNA--Juvenile literature.
Classification: LCC QH437.5 C54 2025 | DDC 572.8--dc23

Alamy: Stocktrek Images Inc 10tr.
Dreamstime: Chemetskaya 18t.
Science Photo Library: A Barrington Brown © Gonville & Caius College 21cr;
CNRI 8c; Valentyna Chukhlyebova 26; Driscoll,Youngquist & Valdeschwiele Caltech 15c; Eye of Science 7br; Pascal Goetcheluck 22; Steve Gschmeissner 5t; Laguna Design 21b, 31b; Science History Images 17c; Volkersteger 25t, 25c.
Shutterstock: AGR211 9tc; AvDe 27b; Birdiegal 23;Simon Bratt 7bc; Roi Brooks 9br; CoreDesign 27t; Cyber Kristiyan 9tl; Evikka 13b;Mila Supinskaya Glashchecko 4c; GUNDAM_Ai 16b; Irin-k 9tr; michael jung 11cl; Just Dance 17t; Ramona Kaulitzki 11t; Lopolo 11b; Brian Mueller 10tc; Mila Naumova 12t; Pixfiction 7c; Susan Schmitz 7bl; sirtravelalot 11cr; Timolina 19b; Surapol USankal 27c; Ustas7777777 20cl; X4wiz 8tl.
Wikimedia Commons: PD 20cr; Kings College, London 21cl.

Printed in the United States of America

CPSIA compliance information: Batch #CSGS25: For further information contact Gareth Stevens at 1-800-542-2595.

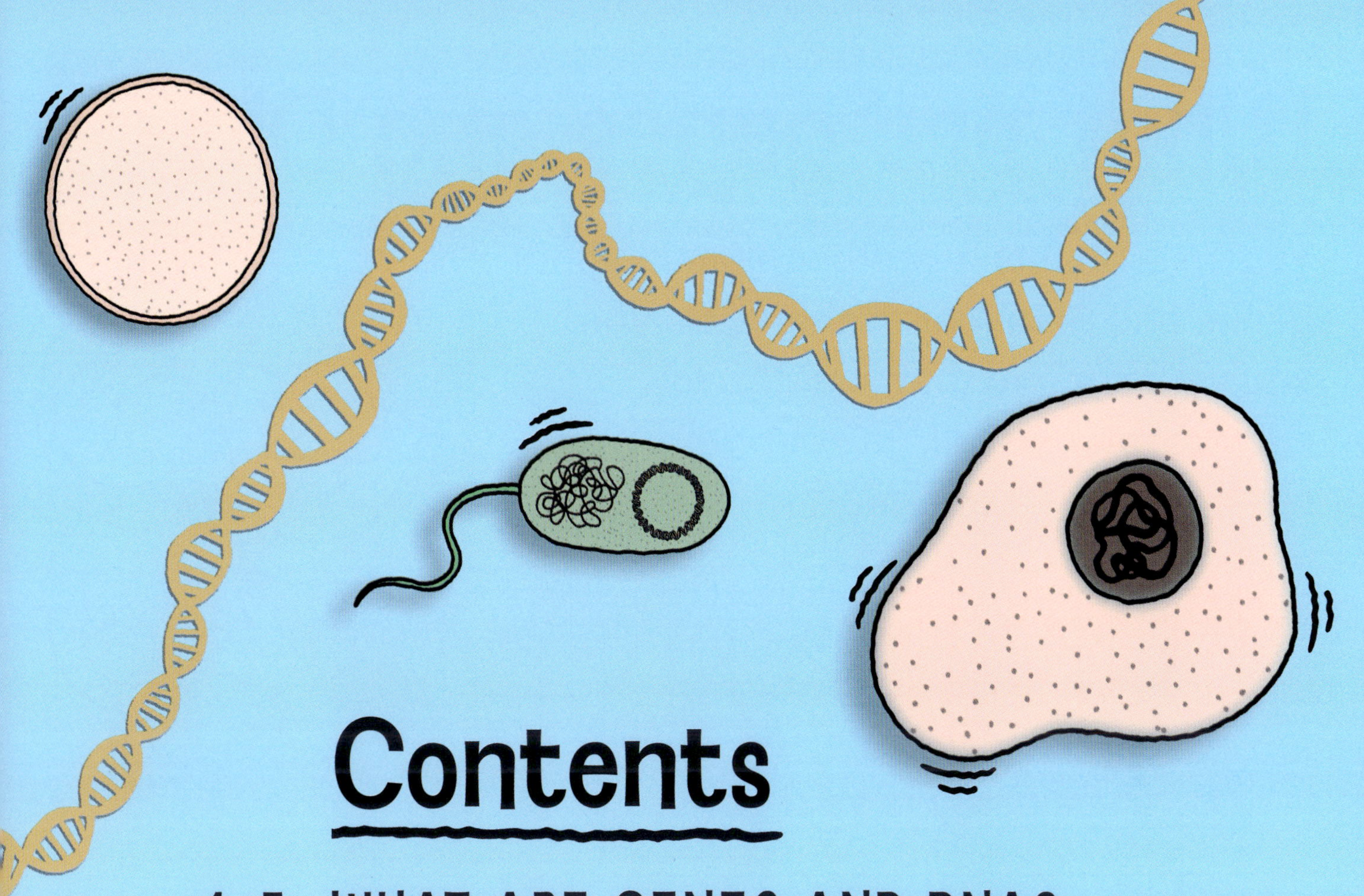

Contents

What are genes and DNA?

You've probably heard people talk about genes and DNA. For example, maybe you've been told that your brown eyes or red hair are "in your genes" and came from your parents.

YOU'VE GOT YOUR DAD'S HAIR!

Even musical or athletic ability can be partly in your genes.

SHE GETS IT FROM ME! IT'S IN OUR DNA.

However ... they don't usually tell you what genes and DNA actually **ARE**, do they?

What are they made of?

?

?

Where are they?

?

How do they work?

?

What does DNA stand for?

Well, this book is going to do that for you! Here goes ...

Let's start with genes ...

Genes are instructions that make cells work.

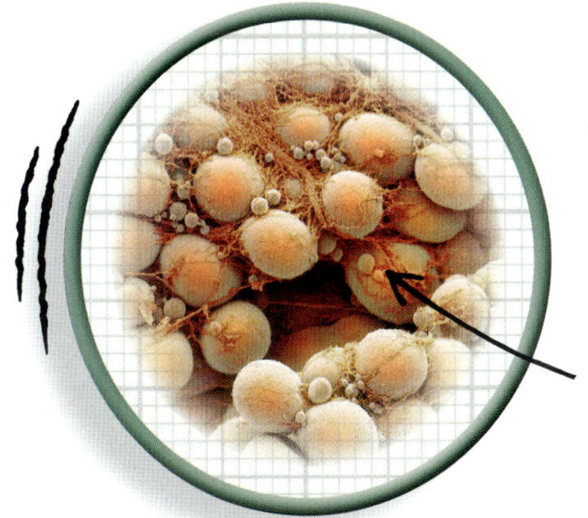

Living things are made up of tiny cells.

Cells under a microscope

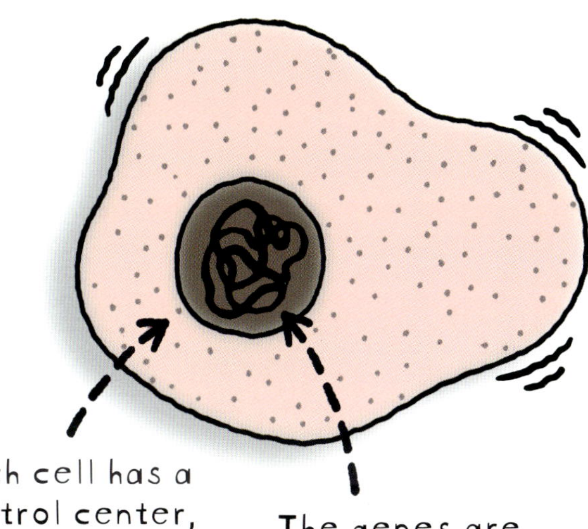

Each cell has a control center, called the nucleus.

The genes are inside the nucleus and tell the cell what to do.

So, what's DNA?

Simple! DNA is what genes are made of. It's a type of chemical.

DNA comes in long strings, or strands.

Genes are sections of DNA.

One gene

Another gene

And DNA stands for ...

DeoxyriboNucleic Acid!

No one wants to keep saying that all the time – so it's DNA for short.

Totally TINY!

Most cells are too small to see. Genes and DNA are inside cells, so they're even tinier.

A strand of DNA is about 2 nanometers wide.

1 nanometer, or nm, is 1 millionth of a mm.

1 mm

That means you could fit 500,000 strands of DNA into 1 mm.

The Tree of Life

All living things have genes and DNA, and they all use the same gene code. This is because we're all related!

The start of life

Life on Earth began around four billion years ago. (How and why, nobody really knows!) The first living thing was probably a simple, single cell, with just a few genes.

When cells copy themselves, they copy their genes. As this happens, "typos" can creep in and genes change or mutate. Gradually, over time, this creates new life-forms.

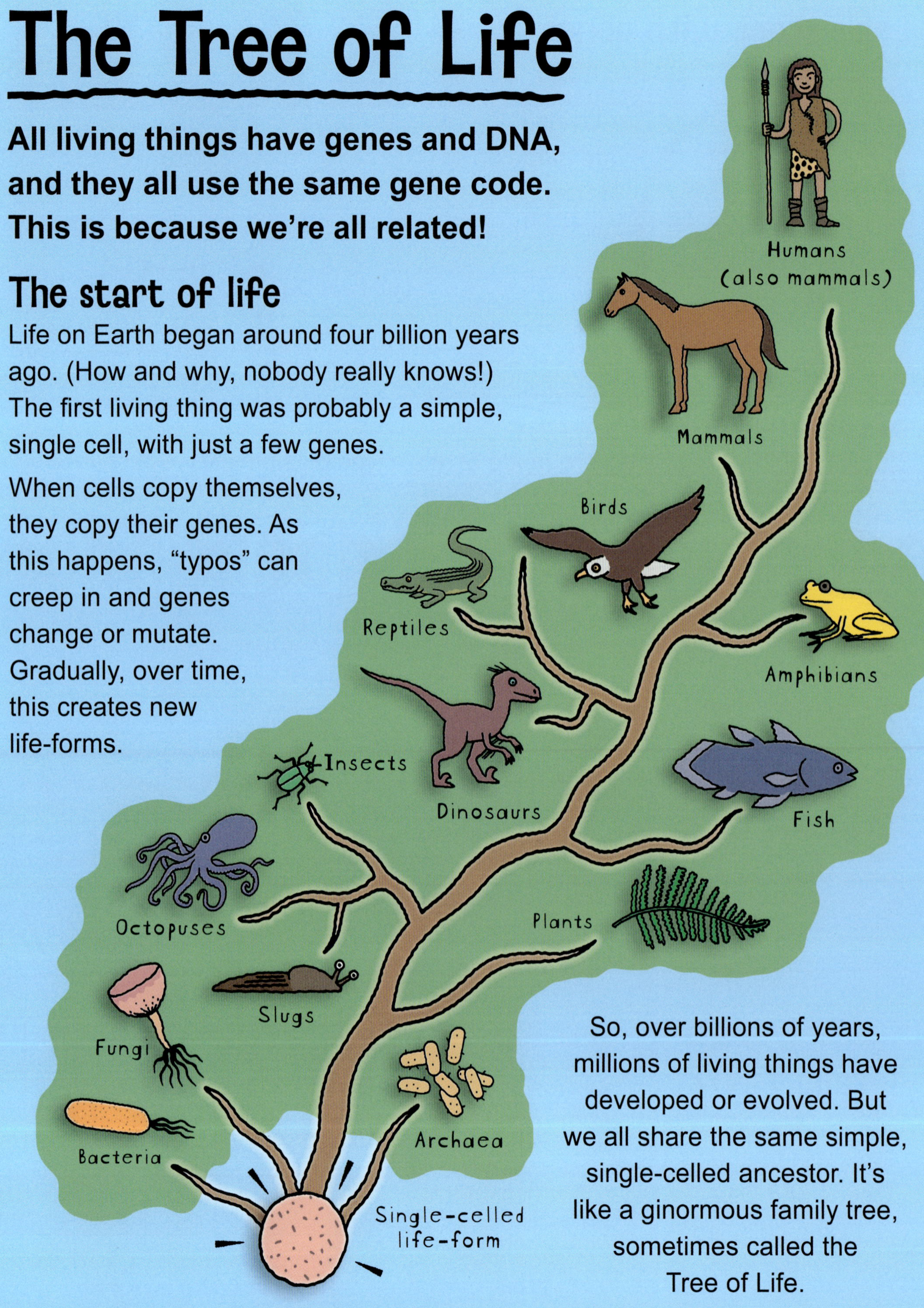

So, over billions of years, millions of living things have developed or evolved. But we all share the same simple, single-celled ancestor. It's like a ginormous family tree, sometimes called the Tree of Life.

That's right – you're not just related to your mom, your cousins, or your great-grandad. You're related to **EVERYTHING** that's alive!

Shared genes

All living things have their own particular set of genes, or genome. But some of the genes are shared and can be found in different living things. You share ...

- 85% with a mouse
- 80% with a cow
- 50% with a banana

Gene recipes

Different species, or types, of living thing have genes that give them all their different shapes, colors, and features – such as wings, fur, tentacles, flowers, or roots. Genes cause all these things ...

Under the microscope

The tiny hairs that make geckos' feet sticky

Flower colors

Stripes on tigers and zebras

A giraffe's long neck

Passing it on

All living things have genes and DNA. But where do they get them? From their parents!

New cells

Reproduction is the process of making new life from bits of existing life. To do this, living things have to make new cells, containing copies of their genes.

A single cell does this by dividing in two.

A bacterium copies its DNA so that it has two sets.

Then it grows and separates ...

... creating two new bacteria, both with the same genes and DNA.

Baby buds

A hydra is a tiny sea creature. It has babies like this ...

The hydra grows some new cells on one side.

They grow into a mini-hydra, or "bud."

The bud breaks off and becomes a baby hydra. It's made of cells from the big hydra and has the same genes.

It takes two

But in humans, cats, birds, flowering plants, and many other species, it takes two cells to make a baby – one male cell and one female cell.

Flower pollen containing male cells joins with female cells in another flower to make seeds, which can grow into baby plants.

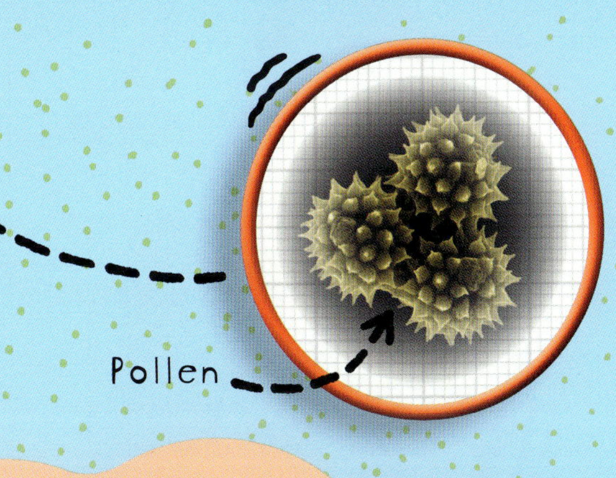

Pollen floats on the wind and can also be carried by insects.

What about us?

Human babies are also made when two cells join together:

A male sperm cell

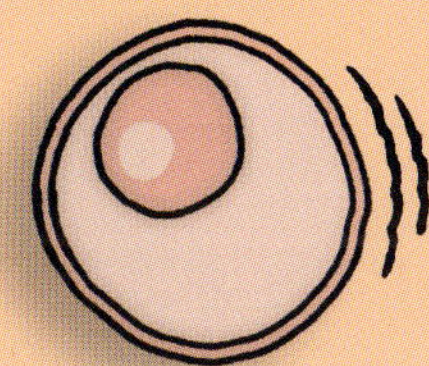

And a female egg cell

This creates a new cell called a zygote, which can grow into a baby.

It contains a mixture of genes from two parents, so it's not an exact copy of either of them.

Mixed genes

Since each person gets their own mix of genes from both parents, everyone is unique.

Human genes

There are about 30,000 genes in the human genome, or full set of genes.

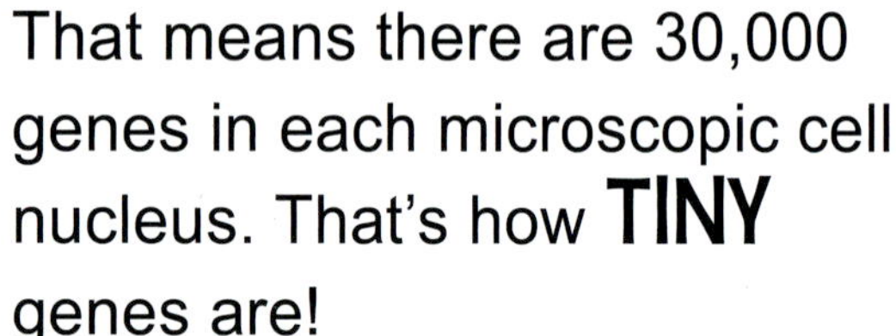

That means there are 30,000 genes in each microscopic cell nucleus. That's how **TINY** genes are!

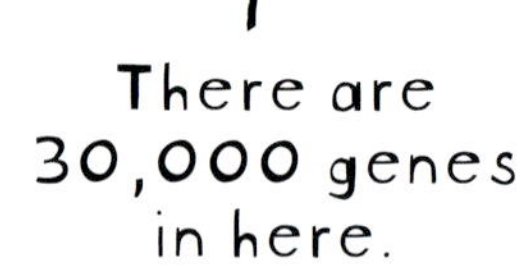

There are 30,000 genes in here.

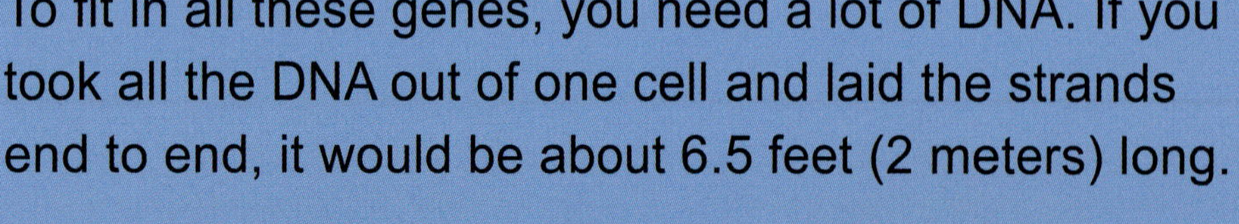

How long is your DNA?

To fit in all these genes, you need a lot of DNA. If you took all the DNA out of one cell and laid the strands end to end, it would be about 6.5 feet (2 meters) long.

You still wouldn't be able to see it, of course, as DNA is very, VERY thin.

To the sun!

So how long is all the DNA in your body? A typical human has around **37 TRILLION** cells (that's 37 million million, or 37,000,000,000,000). However, most of these are red blood cells, which are very small and don't work like other cells. They don't have a cell nucleus or any DNA.

Red blood cells

You have around 3 trillion, or 3,000,000,000,000, DNA-containing cells. All the DNA from these cells added together would be ...

... 3.7 billion miles long.

That's enough to reach from Earth to the sun. And back.

TEN TIMES OVER!

Why are we all different?

If we all have the same 30,000 human genes, why aren't people all the same? Good question!

Although we have the same basic genes, there are differences between them. For example, the genes for hair-making work the same way in everyone, but there are different gene varieties that make different colors of hair. The same goes for eye color, skin color, nose shape, and so on. In fact, everyone* has their own unique genes.

*Even identical twins can have slight variations or mutations in their genes, which form as they grow in the womb – after the single cell separates into two!

What's in your genes?

Lots of things about you are shaped by your genes and DNA. Take a look and see what you've ended up with!

Test your traits

Features like these, which get passed on in genes and DNA, are called genetic traits.

- **Morton's toe**

  Most people's second toes are shorter than their big toes, or the same length. If you have Morton's toe, it means your second toes are extra long and stick out past your big toes.

Morton's toe!

- **Dangly earlobes**

  Your earlobes are the soft parts at the bottom of your ears. Genes control their shape.

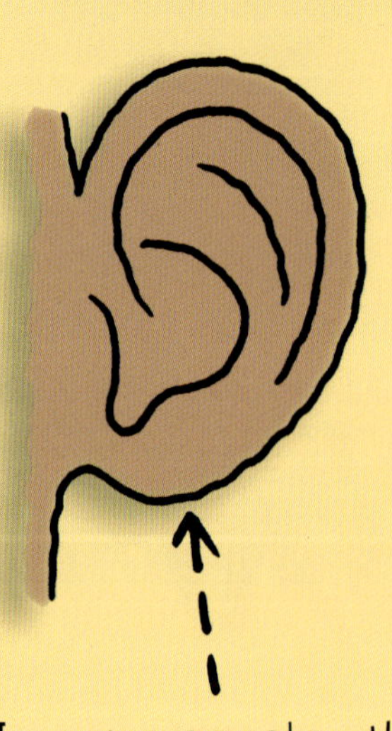

In some people, they join straight onto the side of the head, like this. They're called "attached" earlobes.

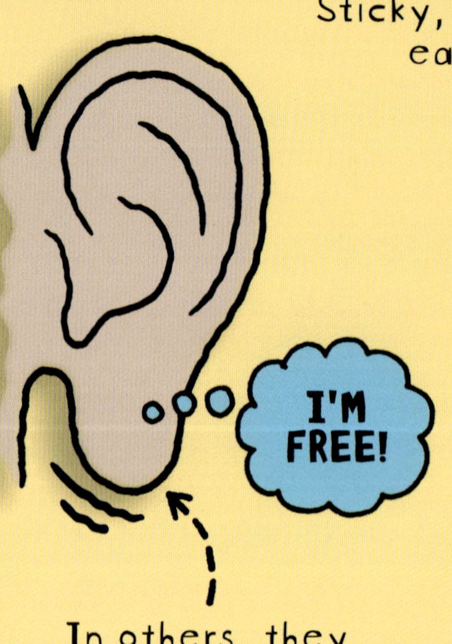

In others, they dangle down and are known as "free" earlobes.

- **Earwax**

  Even your earwax is decided by your genes!

Sensory traits

Genes can also affect how you sense and react to things …

Sneezing in the light

Do you sneeze when you're suddenly hit by bright light? Some people do, some don't – it's in your genes!

Hating sprouts

Some people find the taste of Brussels sprouts, broccoli, and cabbage really bitter and horrible. These people have genes that make them sensitive to a bitter chemical that other people can't taste!

You're not just your genes!

Genes decide lots of things, such as your earlobe shape and eye color – but not everything. Your personality, knowledge, and experiences are important too.

I LOVE CARROTS!

For example, a person's height is partly decided by their genes but also by the food they eat as they grow up. Eating a range of healthy foods can help people reach their fullest height possible.

Inside cells

Let's take a closer look!

Here you can see a bigger picture of a cell, with a view inside the cell nucleus.

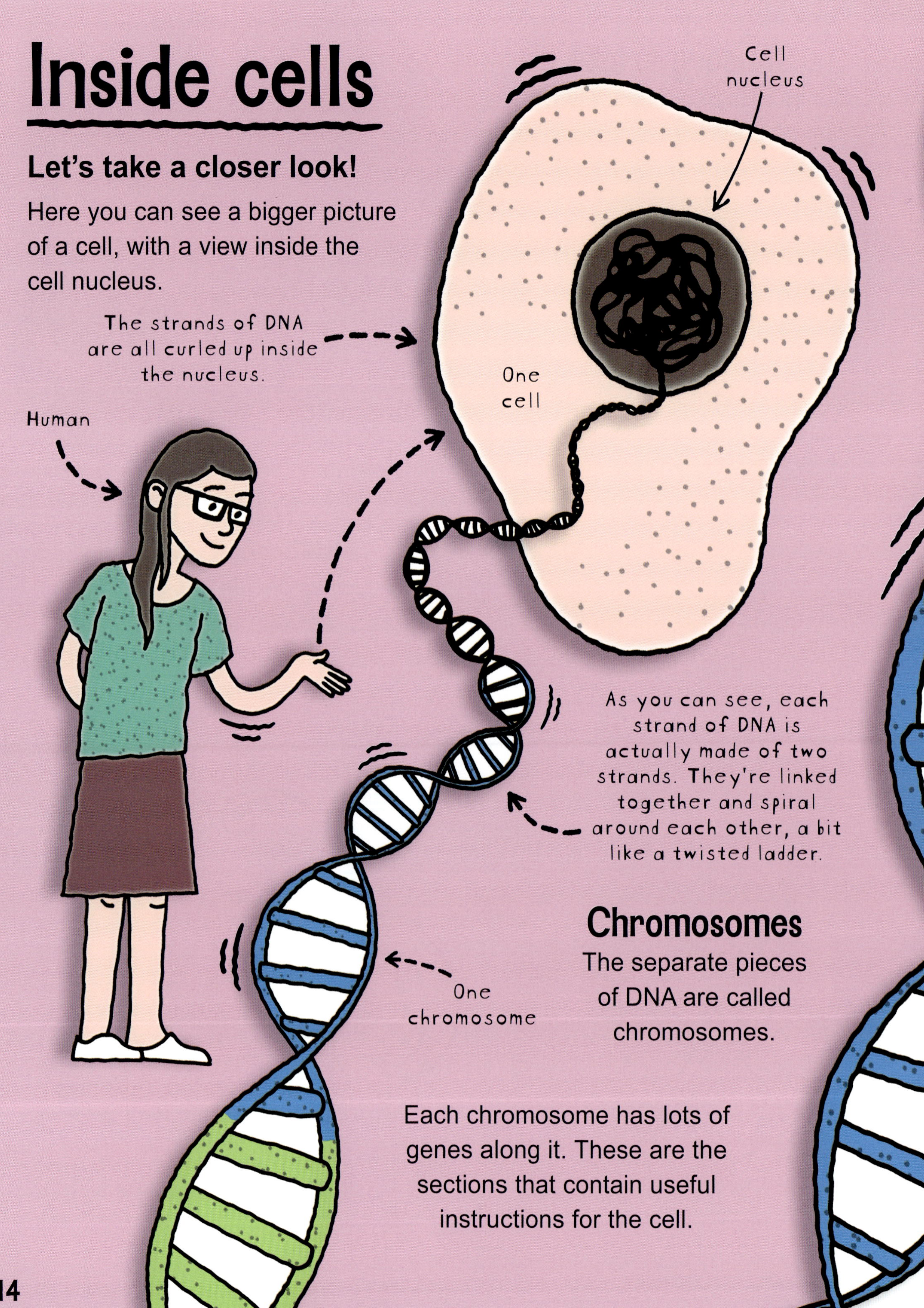

Chromosomes

The separate pieces of DNA are called chromosomes.

Each chromosome has lots of genes along it. These are the sections that contain useful instructions for the cell.

What's this junk?

The parts in between the genes are sometimes called "junk DNA." They're not really junk, though, as they do have some useful jobs, such as helping the DNA coil up into different shapes.

DNA pictures

Although genes and DNA are incredibly tiny, we can see what they look like using powerful modern microscopes.

Under the microscope

Here's a microscope image of an actual DNA strand.

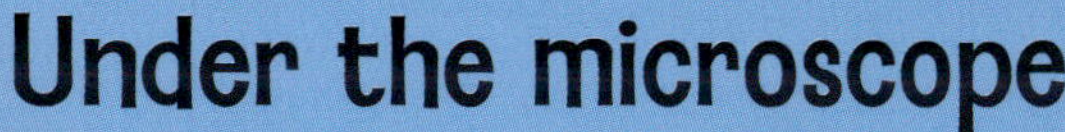

If you look carefully, you can see the spiral shape.

How many chromosomes?

Human cells contain 46 chromosomes, or pieces of DNA.

But this number is different in different living things.

Fruit flies have only 8 chromosomes in each cell.

Spinach plants have 12.

Pet cats have 38.

Great white sharks have 82.

But hang on ...

How can a stringy bit of DNA "tell" a cell what to do? That's what you're wondering, right?

What genes do

ATTENTION, CELLS!

Genes and DNA control what cells do and how they work. But they are not like a boss or an army sergeant giving out orders.

Read the instructions!

Instead, genes contain instructions, written in a kind of code.

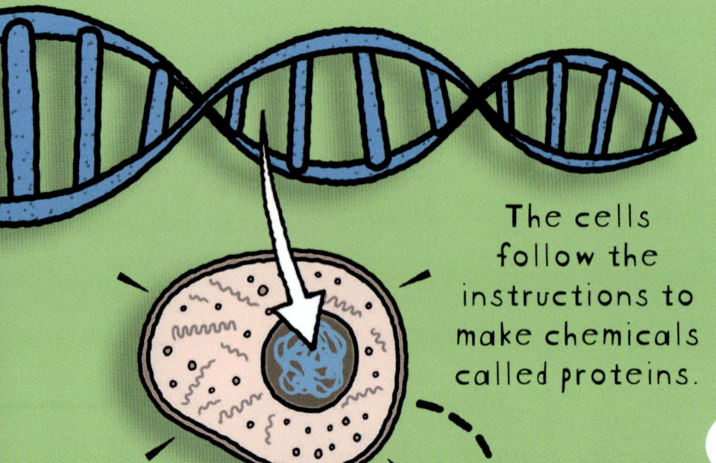

Then the proteins do useful jobs, such as building new cells, growing hair, digesting food, sending signals around your brain, and so on.

Which genes?

Each cell nucleus contains a complete set of human chromosomes or DNA strands. They contain the complete set of genes – or the genome – for that person.

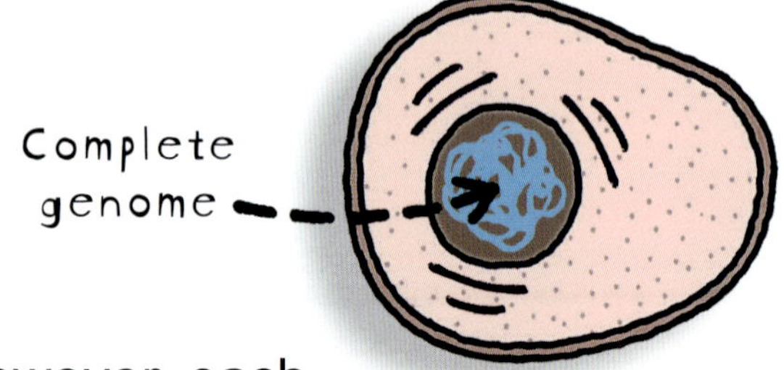

However, each cell uses only some of the genes. For example ...

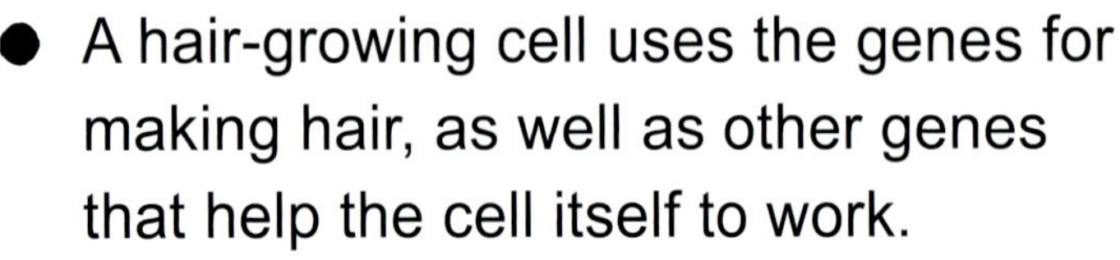

- A hair-growing cell uses the genes for making hair, as well as other genes that help the cell itself to work.
- A cell in your nose uses the genes for making snot.

It's kind of like a recipe book. All your cells contain the whole "book of recipes" – which is the full set of genes – but they use only the "recipes" they need.

On and off

How does a cell know which genes to use? The genes in a cell can be switched on and off so that the cell can only "read" some of them. Scientists are still trying to discover exactly how this works.

GENE SCIENCE IS REALLY HARD!

Missing parts

Sometimes, some of the genes have missing parts, and the cell can't "follow the recipe" properly. This can cause some types of diseases.

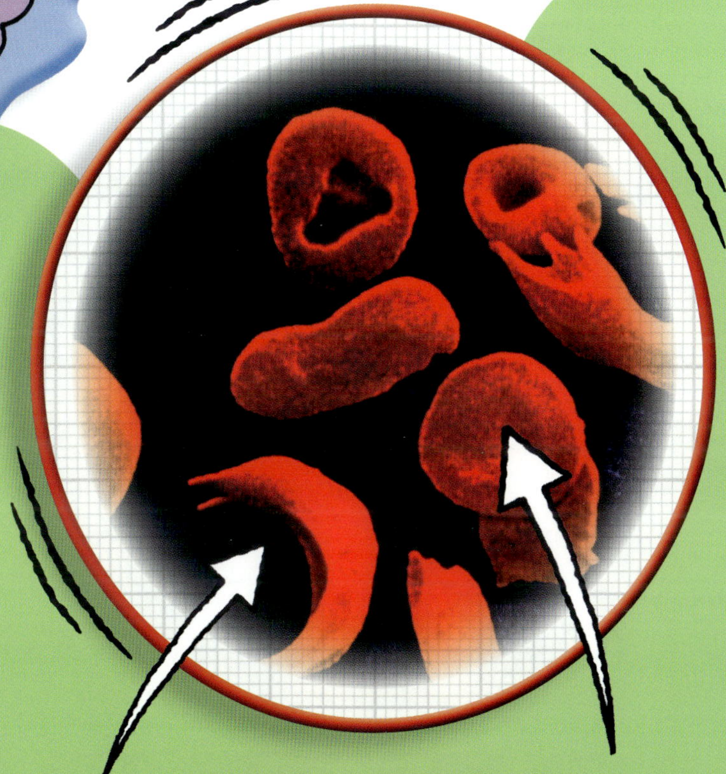

Under the microscope

For example, people with sickle cell anemia have a gene that makes blood cells grow in an unusual shape. Instead of being round, some blood cells are C-shaped, like a tool called a sickle.

This disease can cause pain and make people feel tired and weak.

The gene code

Yes, you read that title right – genes are written in a secret code! Sounds exciting!

Bet you want to see what the code looks like, don't you? Here you go! This is part of a gene that makes keratin, a protein that's used to make hair, skin, and fingernails:

ATGACTACCTGCAGCCGCCAGTTCACCTCCTCCAGCTCCAT GAAGGGCTCCTGCGGCATCGGGGGCGGCATCGGG

What does it mean?

OK, here's how it works ...

DNA contains patterns, made up of four units called bases.

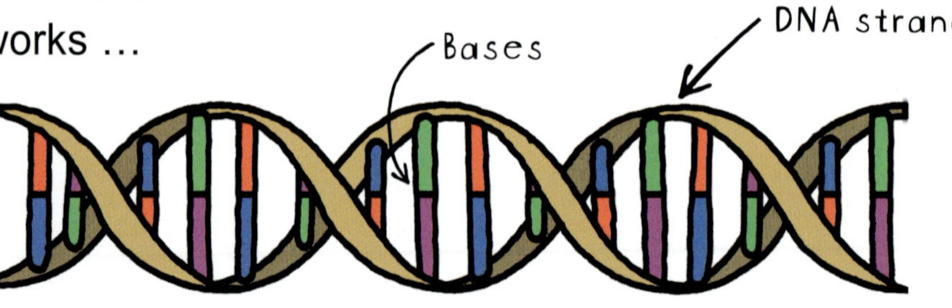

The bases are called adenine, cytosine, guanine, and thymine ...

... or A, C, G, and T for short.

In diagrams, they're shown in different colors.

A  C  G  T 

The four bases fit together in pairs, making up the "rungs" of the DNA ladder.

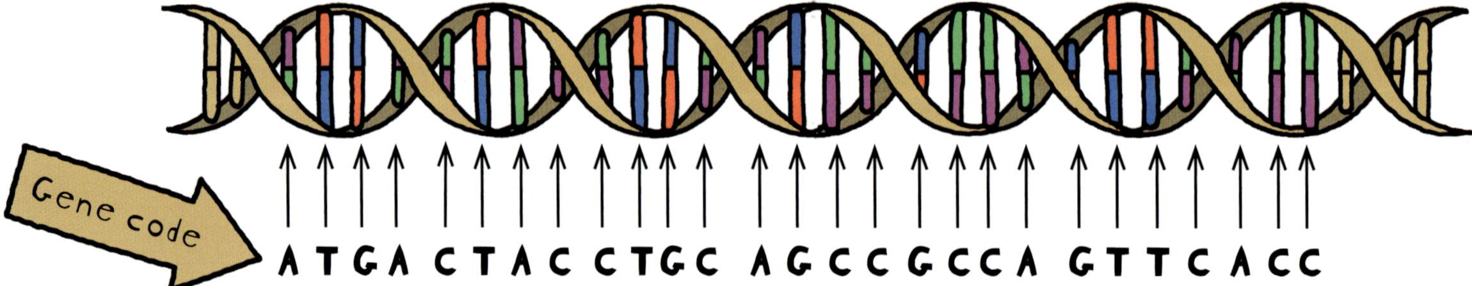

The bases going along ONE SIDE of the ladder are the "letters" of the code.

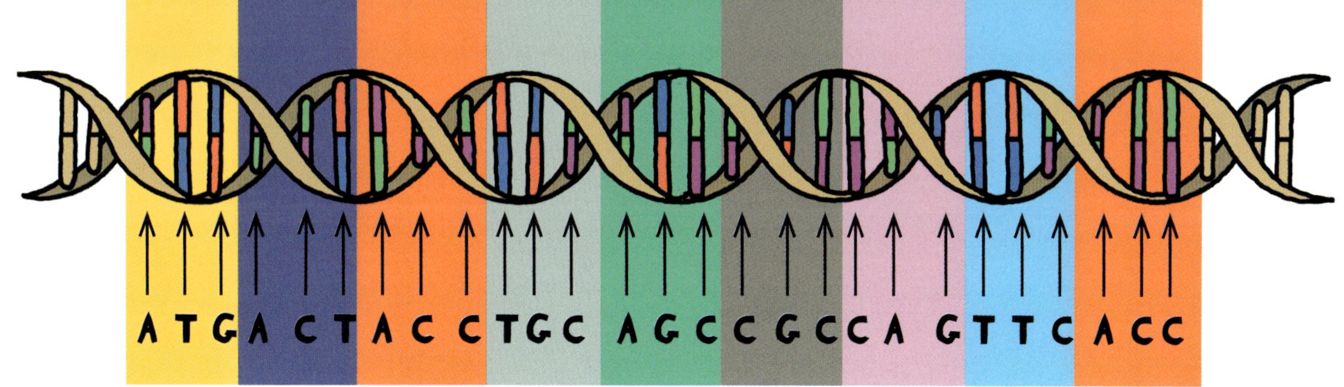

Each group of three bases makes a "code word," called a codon. The codons stand for the different chemicals that cells use to build proteins.

Codon

ATG ACT ACC TGC AGC CGC CAG TTC ACC

Reading the code

To produce proteins, a cell part called a ribosome follows the codons in the gene code, collects the right ingredients, and puts them together in the right order, making a string.

Finally, the string folds up to make the finished protein.

String of chemicals

What are the ingredients?

To do their job making proteins, cells need ingredients – and these come from the food you eat. Your body breaks food down into useful chemicals, and your blood carries them to your cells. They float around inside the cell, waiting to be used.

That's why it's good to eat a wide range of different foods – so your cells have all the right ingredients!

DNA discovery

Follow the timeline to see how we found out about genes and DNA and how they work.

1857–1865
Mendel's garden

Monk and scientist Gregor Mendel studied pea plants in his monastery garden in what is now the Czech Republic. He saw how they passed on traits, such as flower color, in their seeds.

Mendel thought it must be because of something he called "Faktoren," or factors – now known as genes.

HMM, INTERESTING!

1878
Chromosomes in cells

German scientist Walther Flemming used the latest microscopes to study cells as they were dividing and saw chromosomes copying themselves.

Chromosomes

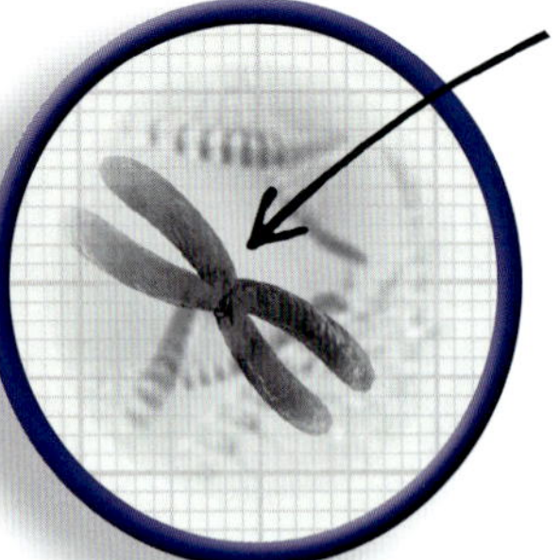

X-shaped chromosomes

When cells get ready to divide, their chromosomes coil up tightly into thick X-like shapes, making them easier to see.

1944
Genes are made of DNA

U.S. scientists Oswald Avery, Colin MacLeod, and Maclyn McCarty found that chromosomes are made of the chemical DNA.

1951
Photo 51

British chemist Rosalind Franklin and her assistant Raymond Gosling used X-rays to make DNA photos. They didn't show DNA itself but the pattern that formed when X-rays shone through it. This famous example, "Photo 51," showed that DNA has a spiral shape.

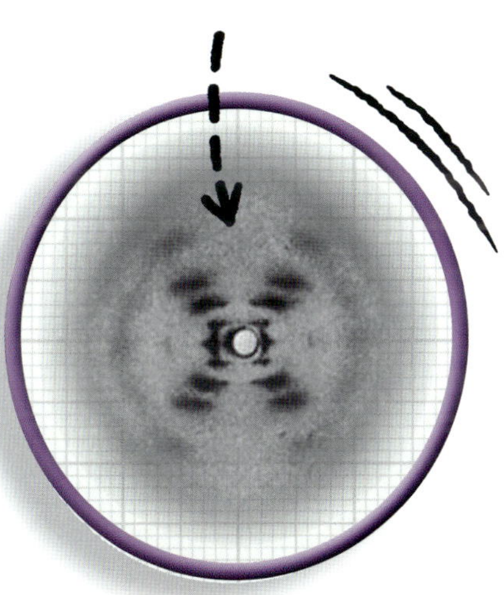

1953
Watson and Crick

These photos helped two other scientists, American James Watson and Francis Crick of Britain, find the structure of DNA. They built this model of it.

1960s onward

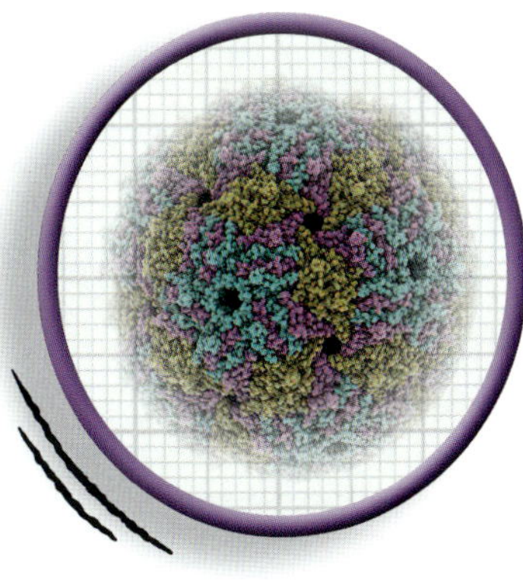

Many scientists worked on understanding the gene code and figuring out the genomes of living things.

Still working on it!

There's still a lot to learn about genes and DNA, and scientists around the world are studying them and finding out new things.

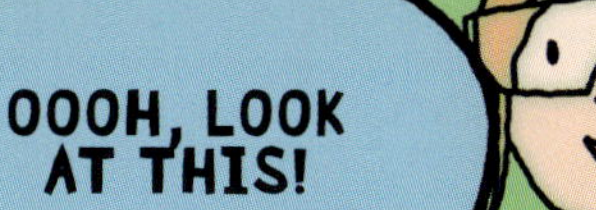

DNA detectives

Everyone has their own unique DNA patterns – and that means DNA can be used to identify people.

DNA fingerprinting

DNA fingerprinting is a way of using someone's DNA to make a pattern. Just like real fingerprints, it can be used to catch criminals.

Here's how ...

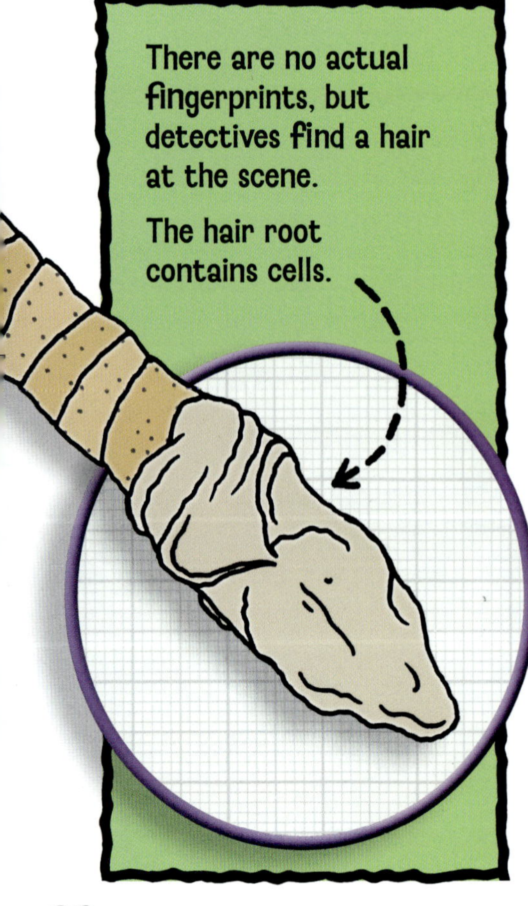

The pieces are passed through a special gel, which makes them spread out. This makes a pattern of marks, called a DNA fingerprint.

DNA from crime scene

When the detectives arrest Nick, they test his DNA and compare it to the DNA from the crime scene. If they match, he was there!

What else?

DNA tests can also reveal …

- Just how closely related people are – because close relatives have similar patterns
- Whether you have a disease caused by DNA
- Who your ancestors were – for example, if you're partly Viking, Aztec, or Neanderthal.

This could be your ancestor.

Nature detectives

Plants, animals, and other living things can have their DNA tested too.

In the past, no one was sure what type of animal the giant panda was. Some scientists thought it was related to raccoons. Now, DNA testing shows it really belongs to the bear family.

Changing genes

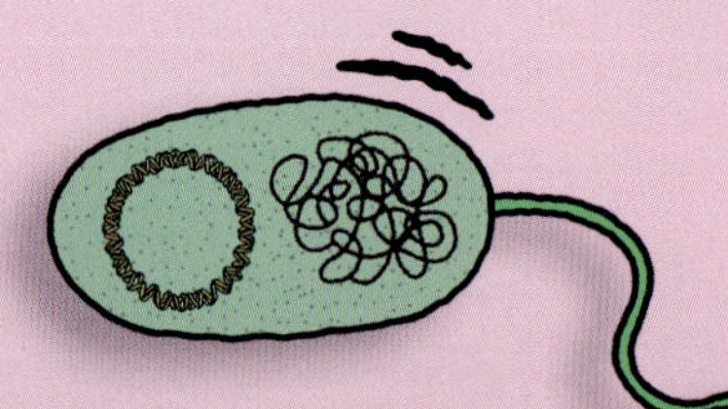

That's right – scientists can actually take a cell or a living thing and change its genes to make it work differently. It's often called genetic modification, or GM.

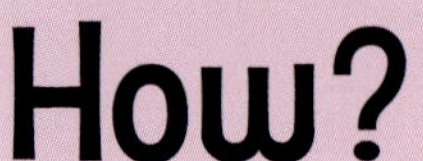

How?

There are several ways of doing this. Here's one!

1. Here's a single-celled bacterium. Like other living things, it uses its genes to make proteins.

2. It has a small loop of DNA called a plasmid. Scientists can take this out ...

3. ... use an enzyme protein to cut it ...

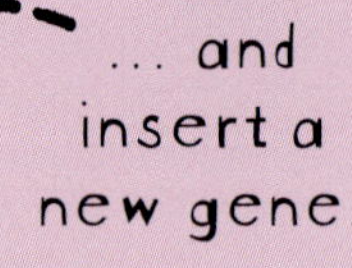

4. ... and insert a new gene.

5. Then they put it back in ...

6. ... and the gene tells the bacterium to start making a new protein.

7. When the bacterium divides to make more bacteria, they all have the new gene.

Why do we do it?

GM has lots of uses. For example, people with the disease diabetes need injections of insulin. We make GM bacteria that produce lots of insulin, then collect it for diabetics to use.

GM bacteria

Under the microscope

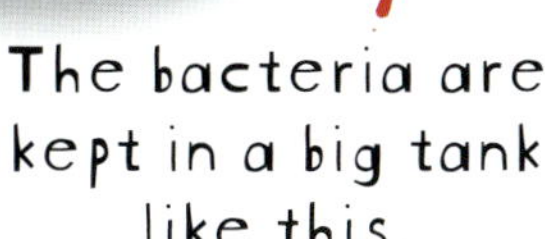

The bacteria are kept in a big tank like this.

GM has also been used ...

- To make crops that survive frost, repel pest insects, or grow more fruit.
- To make farm animals, such as pigs, that are less likely to get illnesses.
- To make cows fart and burp less so they release less methane, which is a cause of global warming!

Isn't it dangerous?

Some people worry that GM could cause problems. What if we accidentally created a deadly disease? Or a monster animal?

There are strict rules and safety tests to avoid this, but some people still don't agree with it.

Could we make GM people?

It's possible that GM could be used in people, for example to cure some types of diseases. But scientists agree we should be VERY careful!

Gene inventions

Gene scientists are working on all kinds of new ways to use genes and DNA. Some are happening now, and some could come along in the future.

Cloning

A clone is an exact copy of a living thing. It happens naturally all the time. For example, the hydra bud on page 8 is a clone of its parent.

But scientists have now used DNA to clone bigger animals. In 1996, they created the first cloned sheep.

HELLO AGAIN!

Back from extinction

Another use for cloning could be to bring extinct species back to life. For example, DNA from a frozen extinct mammoth could be used to grow a cloned baby mammoth inside a female elephant.

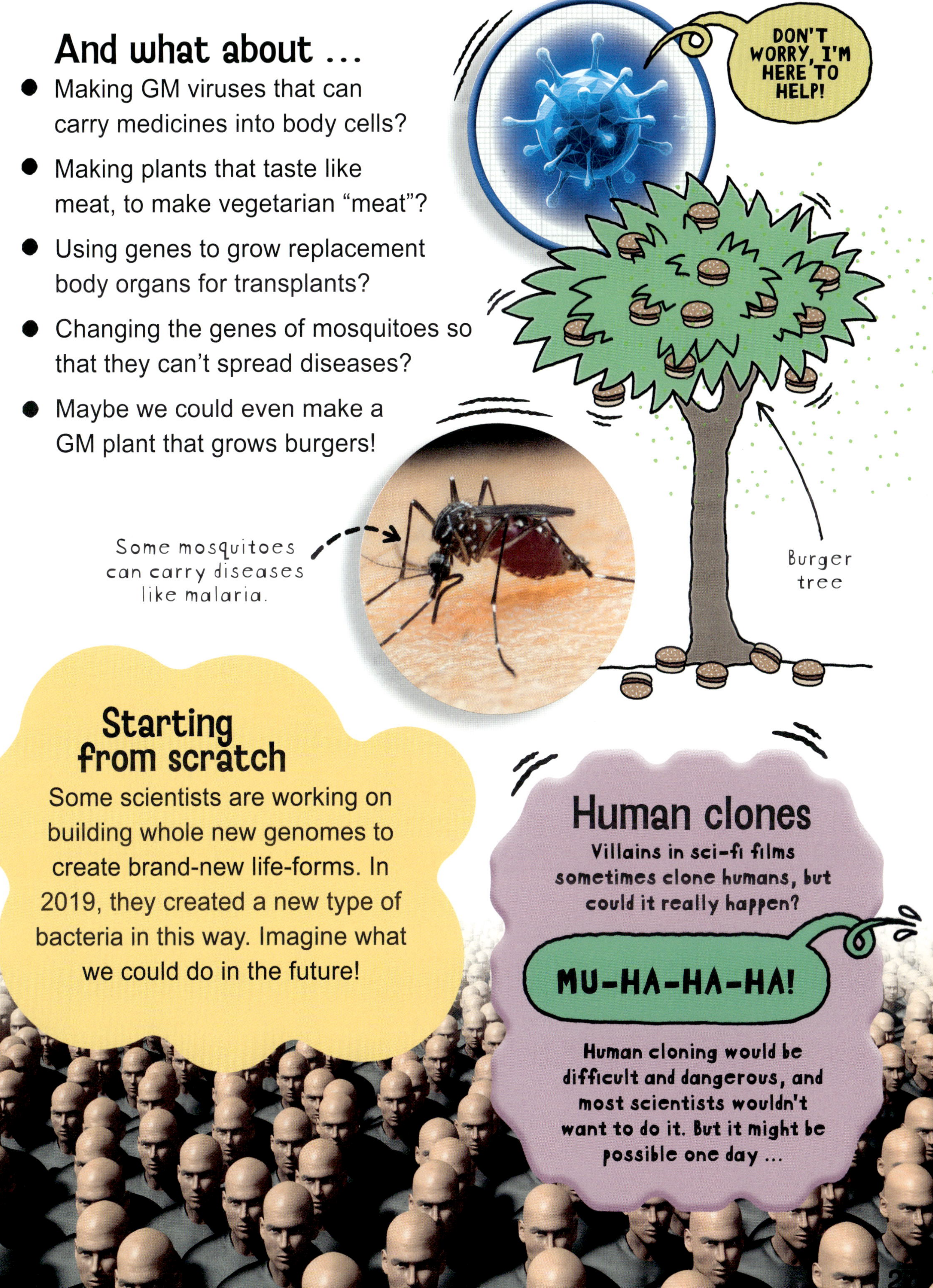

And what about ...

- Making GM viruses that can carry medicines into body cells?
- Making plants that taste like meat, to make vegetarian "meat"?
- Using genes to grow replacement body organs for transplants?
- Changing the genes of mosquitoes so that they can't spread diseases?
- Maybe we could even make a GM plant that grows burgers!

Starting from scratch

Some scientists are working on building whole new genomes to create brand-new life-forms. In 2019, they created a new type of bacteria in this way. Imagine what we could do in the future!

Human clones

Villains in sci-fi films sometimes clone humans, but could it really happen?

Human cloning would be difficult and dangerous, and most scientists wouldn't want to do it. But it might be possible one day ...

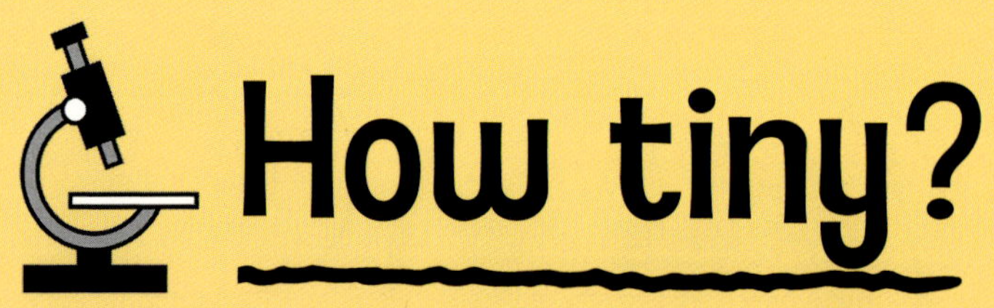

How tiny?

As you know, genes and DNA are very, very, VERY small! So small, it's hard to imagine. This picture shows some of the tiny things in this book compared to one another, to help you get a good idea of their size.

Micro measures

For measuring normal everyday things, we use centimeters, inches, meters, or feet. But for much smaller things like cells, scientists use the micron (or micrometer).

One micron is 1,000th of a millimeter.

So there are 1,000 microns in a millimeter... and 1 million microns in a meter.

The micron symbol is:

µm

Human hair

A human hair, for example, is around 80 µm thick.

And for even tinier things like DNA, they use the nanometer.

One nanometer is 1,000th of a micrometer – or one millionth of a millimeter.

The nanometer symbol is

nm.

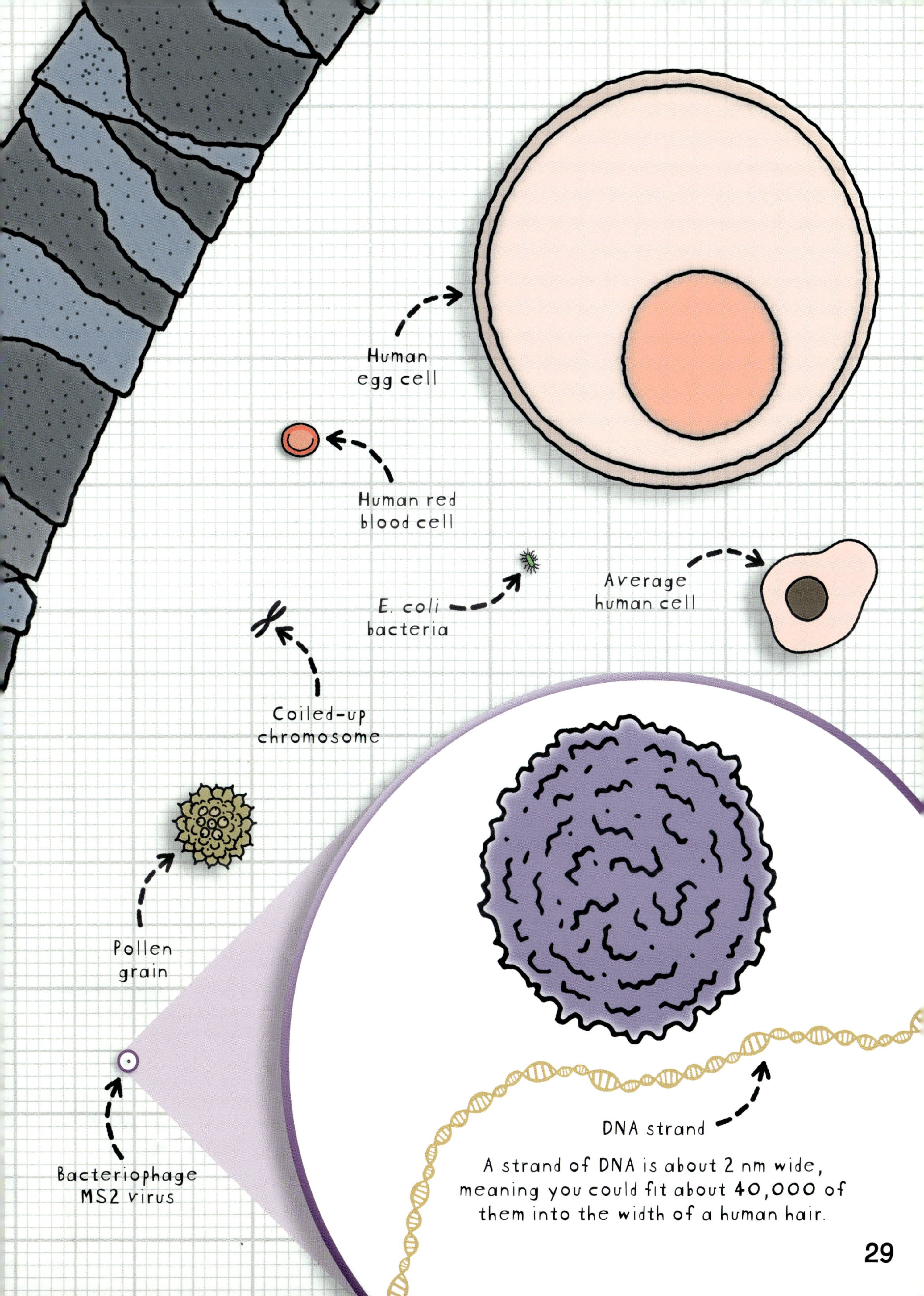
Human egg cell
Human red blood cell
E. coli bacteria
Average human cell
Coiled-up chromosome
Pollen grain
Bacteriophage MS2 virus
DNA strand
A strand of DNA is about 2 nm wide, meaning you could fit about 40,000 of them into the width of a human hair.

Glossary

ancestor A relative who lived a long time before you, such as your great-great-great-great-grandma.

bacteria A type of very small single-celled living thing.

bases Four chemicals that are arranged in different patterns in DNA, making the gene code.

bud A type of baby living thing that grows from one side of its parent, then breaks off.

cells The tiny building blocks that make up living things.

chromosomes The separate strands of DNA found inside cells.

clone A living thing that is an exact copy of another living thing.

codon A group of three bases in the gene code.

diabetes An illness that makes it hard for the body to control the amount of sugar in the blood.

DNA (Short for deoxyribonucleic acid) String-shaped chemical that genes are made of.

DNA fingerprinting Using patterns from a person's DNA to identify them.

egg cell A female cell that can join with a sperm cell to make a zygote, which can grow into a new living thing.

enzyme A type of natural protein. Some enzymes can cut DNA strands into shorter pieces.

evolve The way species of living things gradually change over time.

gene code The coded information that tells cells what to do, written in genes as a pattern of bases.

genetic To do with genes.

genetic modification (GM) Changing one or more of a living thing's genes to change the way it grows or lives.

genetic traits Body shapes, abilities, or other features caused by genes.

genome The complete set of genes for a particular living thing.

germs Tiny living things that can cause diseases in other living things.

global warming An increase in Earth's average temperature, caused by human activities.

GM Short for genetic modification.

hydra A type of very small, simple sea animal.

insulin A body chemical that helps to control the amount of sugar in the blood.

junk DNA The sections of DNA between the genes – although they are not actually junk, but do useful jobs.

malaria A disease spread by mosquitoes that can be deadly.

methane A gas that helps to cause global warming, released from farm animals like cows and also when things decay.

micrometer Another name for a micron.

micron A tiny unit of measurement, one-thousandth of a millimeter long.

nanometer An extremely tiny unit of measurement, equal to one-thousandth of a micrometer or one-millionth of a millimeter.

Neanderthal A different species of human from us that became extinct around 40,000 years ago.

nucleus A part found in some cells that contains the cell's genes and DNA.

organ A body part that does a special job, such as the stomach, liver, heart, or lungs.

organ transplant Replacing a diseased or damaged organ with a healthy one.

plasmid A small, usually loop-shaped piece of DNA often found in bacteria, which is separate from the rest of a bacterium's DNA.

pollen A powdery yellow substance released by plants, containing male cells needed to make seeds.

protein A type of chemical found in living things, used to build body parts and do other jobs in the body.

red blood cell A type of blood cell that carries oxygen around the body.

species A particular type of living thing.

sperm cell A male cell that can join with an egg cell to make a zygote, which can grow into a new living thing.

virus A type of very small germ that can invade living cells and use them to make copies of itself. Some viruses cause diseases.

zygote A new cell made when a sperm cell and an egg cell join together and that can grow into a new living thing.

Further information

Websites

www.amnh.org/explore/ology/genetics#all

Genes and DNA games, facts, videos, and activities from the American Museum of Natural History.

www.bbc.co.uk/bitesize/topics/zpffr82/articles/zvwbcj6

Info, video, and quiz from BBC Bitesize.

dnalc.cshl.edu/resources/3d/23-dna-unzip.html

3D animation showing DNA being straightened out and taken apart, so you can see how it works.

https://www.unlockinglifescode.org/media-gallery/animated-genome

"The Animated Genome," a fun video explaining DNA facts.

Books

The Secret Code Inside You: All About Your DNA

By Rajani LaRocca and Steven Salerno (Little Bee Books, 2021)

The DNA Book: Discover What Makes You You

By Alison Woollard and Sophie Gilbert (Dorling Kindersley, 2020)

Grow: Secrets of Our DNA

By Nicola Davies and Emily Sutton (Walker Books, 2021)

My First Book About Genetics

By Patricia J. Wynne and Donald Silver (Dover Children's Science Books, 2018)

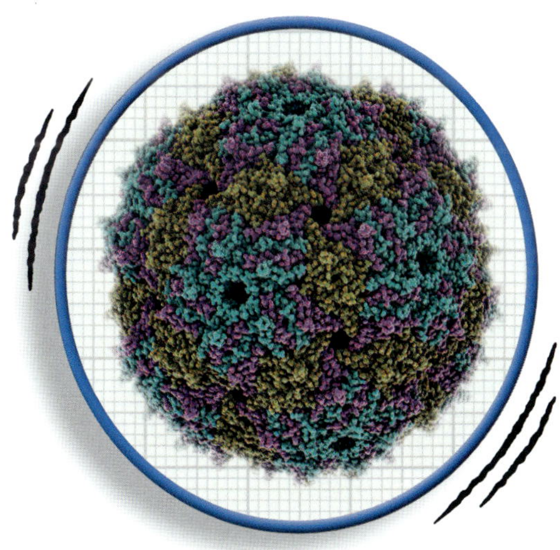

Every effort has been made by the Publishers to ensure that the websites in this book are suitable for children, that they are of the highest educational value, and that they contain no inappropriate or offensive material. However, because of the nature of the Internet, it is impossible to guarantee that the contents of these sites will not be altered. We strongly advise that Internet access is supervised by a responsible adult.

Index